ENTER the DRAGON
SCRAPBOOK SEQUENCES
volume one

Bruce Lee is without doubt one of the most photographed movie stars in the world. There are tens of thousands of images, both on set and off, capturing Bruce in his everyday life weather he is training, at a function, home with his family or socialising with friends. But without doubt there is an incredible amount of photos of Bruce when he is filming. With each movie came more photographs, Bruce himself was a keen photographer, and always wanted to check any photos that were taken of him often taken by his regular cameraman "Chan Yuk to make sure the best images were used for publicity shots So, by the time "Enter the Dragon" went into production there was a multitude of both cameramen shooting behind the scenes and photographers making ETD the most photographed of all of Bruce's film. I estimate that there is probably over 9000 plus from that movie alone. Back then the photographer would snap 36 shots in succession to capture Bruce's art form and lightning speed so they could ensure that some of the shots would be useable. This scrapbook takes some of those sequences capturing the many emotions of Bruce both on screen and behind the scenes.

We have used some rare images twhere the contact sheet has been damaged over time and been scratched but have kept them in for your pleasure as these would not be suitable for quality printing but ideal to show case in this scrapbook.

Also available

Volume two

www.ingramcontent.com/pod-product-compliance
Lightning Source LLC
Chambersburg PA
CBHW042019090526
44590CB00029B/4340